UNDER OCCUPATION

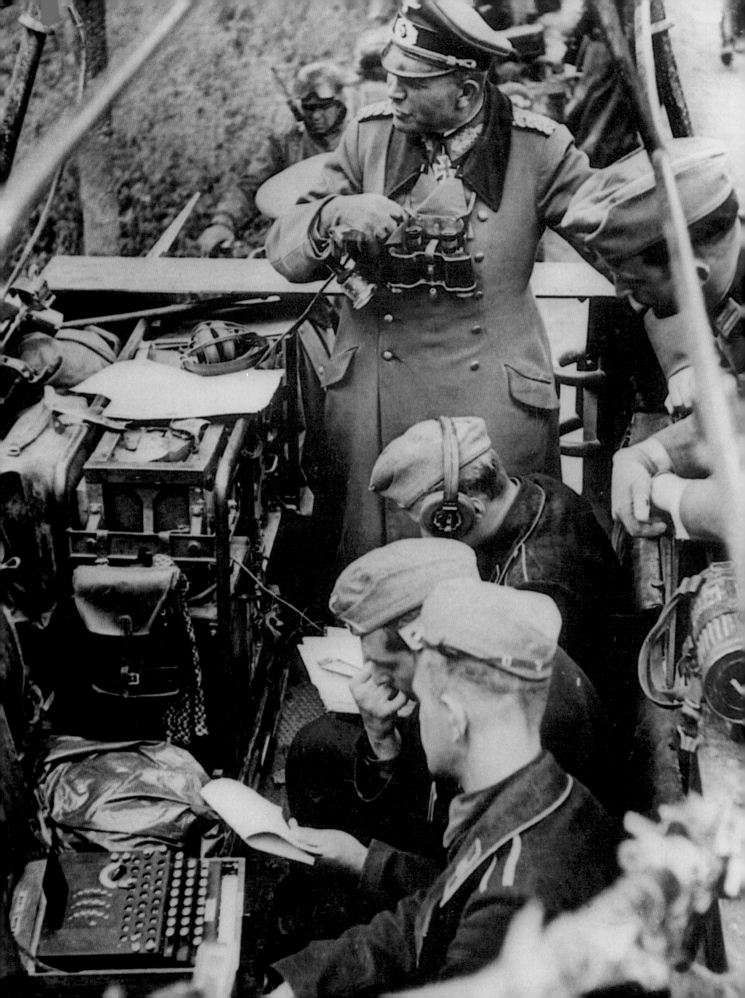

UNDER OCCUPATION

SIMON ADAMS

FRANKLIN WATTS
LONDON•SYDNEY

Designer Jason Billin
Editor Jennifer Schofield
Art Director Jonathan Hair
Editor-in-Chief John C. Miles
Picture research Diana Morris

© 2005 Franklin Watts

First published in 2005
by Franklin Watts
96 Leonard Street
London EC2A 4XD

Franklin Watts Australia
Level 17/207 Kent Street
Sydney NSW 2000

ISBN 0 7496 6360 X

A CIP catalogue record for this book
is available from the British Library.

Printed in China

Dewey classification number: 940.53'36

Picture credits
AKG Images: 22
Cody Images: 2, 7, 8, 13, 14, 16, 19,
28, 29, 31, 32
PA/Topham: 17
Picturepoint/Topham: front cover b,
back cover b, 12, 20, 21, 24, 27, 30
Roger-Viollet/Topham: front cover t,
back cover t, 11

*Every attempt has been made to
clear copyright. Should there be any
inadvertent omission please apply to the
publisher for rectification.*

Note to parents and teachers:
Every effort has been made by the Publishers
to ensure that the websites in this book are
suitable for children, that they are of the
highest educational value, and that they
contain no inappropriate or offensive
material. However, because of the nature of
the Internet, it is impossible to guarantee
that the contents of these sites will not be
altered. We strongly advise that Internet
access is supervised by a responsible adult.

CONTENTS

Introduction

During World War II, between 1939 and 1945, many countries in Europe and eastern Asia were occupied by Germany, Italy and Japan. This book is about those countries and how their people coped with life under occupation.

The Origins of World War II

World War II began in September 1939, when Germany invaded Poland. Britain and France supported Poland, and so declared war against Germany. The war soon spread around the world as other countries joined in on one side or the other, or were invaded. But the origins of the war go back much further than 1939, back to World War I, which was fought between 1914 and 1918.

At the end of World War I, Germany was defeated by Britain, France, the USA and their allies. In June 1919, at Versailles in France, Germany had to agree to harsh peace terms, which it bitterly resented. Italy and Japan were on the winning side in the war, but both felt that the peace treaty did not give them enough status and new territory in reward. All three nations – Germany, Italy and Japan – felt cheated by the peace settlement, and increasingly worked together to overthrow it.

The Occupying Nations

Italy was ruled by the fascist government of Benito Mussolini (1883–1945). Fascists believed in nationalism and authority, and aimed to unite a country's people under an all-powerful leader.

Germany was led by Adolf Hitler (1889–1945), whose Nazi Party developed an even more extreme version of fascism. Nazis were anti-Semitic and believed that the Germans were a "master race" who would dominate the world.

Between 1922 and 1945, fascism flourished in Italy, Spain, Germany, Austria, Croatia and much of eastern Europe. Japan, although fascist in many ways, was increasingly run as a dictatorship by its military leaders.

World Domination

The three nations also turned their backs on democracy and became dictatorships (see fact box). They wanted to acquire large territorial and economic empires – Germany in Europe, Italy around the Mediterranean Sea and in Africa, and Japan in eastern Asia and the Pacific – and between them dominate the world. In 1936–37 the three formed a powerful alliance, known as the Axis. By the outbreak of World War II in 1939, all three had already acquired much new territory – Germany in Austria and Czechoslovakia, Italy in Ethiopia and Albania, Japan in China – and were preparing to acquire much more.

Occupied Countries

Occupied by Germany

1938 Austria, Sudeten border region of Czechoslovakia

1939 Bohemia and Moravia (western Czechoslovakia), Poland

1940 Denmark, Norway, Netherlands, Belgium, Luxembourg, northern France, Channel Islands (part of UK)

1941 Yugoslavia, Greece, western Russia, Belarus, Ukraine, the Baltic states (Estonia, Latvia, Lithuania)

1942 Vichy France

1944 Hungary

Occupied by Italy

1936 Ethiopia

1939 Albania

Occupied by Japan

1931 Manchuria (a province of northern China)

1937 Eastern China

1941 Hong Kong, Malaya, Brunei

1942 Singapore, Indonesia, Burma, Philippines, New Guinea, Solomon Islands

A German Heinkel aircraft drops bombs on Poland, September 1939.

Governing Occupied Europe

When the German and Italian armies invaded and occupied a country, new governments had to be set up. These governments varied enormously, but they all obeyed orders from either Berlin or Rome.

Governments in Exile

Many heads of state whose countries were invaded by Germany fled to Britain. By 1941, the kings and queens of Norway, the Netherlands, Luxembourg, Yugoslavia and Greece, the president of Czechoslovakia, the prime minister of Belgium, the former prime minister of Poland, and the leader of the Free French (General Charles de Gaulle) all lived in London.

They all formed governments in exile, which were supported by Britain with financial help, accommodation, and access to BBC radio to broadcast to their people – and their resistance fighters – at home. All prepared for the day when their countries would be liberated and they could return home once again.

Once it had occupied Norway, Germany allowed Nazi sympathiser Vidkun Quisling to become prime minister. After the war he was tried and executed.

Occupation

By the end of 1941, the whole of Europe was under German or Italian control except for Britain, which fought on alone against Germany after the defeat of France in May 1940. Five states remained neutral: Ireland, Portugal, Spain, Sweden and Switzerland. Five other states, including Hungary and Romania, were allied to Germany and worked with it.

Large parts of Europe were swallowed whole by the invading countries – Germany incorporated Austria, Bohemia and Moravia (western Czechoslovakia), and most of Poland into the *Grossdeutsches Reich* (Greater Germany), and divided Yugoslavia and Greece with Italy. Elsewhere, a variety of different governments were installed.

Collaboration

In some countries, the Germans allowed local pro-Nazi sympathisers to set up their own governments of collaboration. The former war minister and Nazi sympathiser, Vidkun Quisling, became prime minister of Norway, while the Yugoslav province of Croatia was led by a pro-German fascist government, although it remained under effective German and Italian military control because of the activities of the partisans (see pages 14–15). In unoccupied (Vichy) France, General Pétain led a collaborationist government (see pages 10–11). Uniquely, King Christian X and his ministers stayed in power in Denmark, although they refused to carry out German orders and were eventually removed from power in 1943.

Civilian or Military Rule?

Elsewhere, the Germans imposed their own civilian governments run by German officials, notably in the Netherlands, where Arthur Seyss-Inquart, former chancellor (prime minister) of Austria, became Reich Commissioner.

In most places, however, civilian government was impossible because the area was of too much military importance to Germany. Both Belgium and northern France were therefore under German military control because of fears that Britain might invade them across the English Channel, while military governments ran almost all the occupied regions of the Soviet Union.

But whatever the type of government, it was always clear that the Germans were in charge, and that resistance to their rule would be met with violence and repression.

Occupation Governments in Europe

AUSTRIA, BOHEMIA AND MORAVIA, LUXEMBOURG, WESTERN POLAND United with Germany as part of the Grossdeutsches Reich.

BALTIC STATES, BELARUS German civilian government.

BELGIUM, EASTERN POLAND, OCCUPIED RUSSIA, UKRAINE, EASTERN YUGOSLAVIA, NORTHERN GREECE AND CRETE German military government.

DENMARK Self-government under King Christian X.

FRANCE Occupied zone under German military government (also controlled the British-owned Channel Islands). Vichy France led by pro-German government of General Pétain.

NETHERLANDS German civilian government led by Reich Commissioner Arthur Seyss-Inquart.

NORWAY Pro-German government led by Norwegian collaborator Vidkun Quisling.

ALBANIA, SOUTHERN GREECE, WESTERN YUGOSLAVIA United with Italy.

BULGARIA, FINLAND, HUNGARY, ROMANIA, SLOVAKIA Independent states closely allied to Germany and often taking orders from it.

France Under Occupation

In May 1940, Germany began the invasion of western Europe. Within six weeks, German troops had occupied the Netherlands, Belgium, Luxembourg, and France. For the French, defeat was a national catastrophe.

General Pétain

General Henri-Philippe Pétain (1856–1951) joined the French army in 1878. He became a national hero in 1916 when he organised the defence of Verdun against German attack, raising morale with his cry: *"Ils ne passeront pas!"* (They shall not pass!). He left the army after the war but in May 1940 as German armies threatened France, he came out of retirement to join the government.

On 16 June 1940, he became prime minister and agreed peace terms with Germany six days later. Pétain collaborated with the Germans as leader of unoccupied Vichy France, but became a mere figurehead when they occupied the whole of France in November 1942. After the war, he was found guilty of treason and sentenced to life imprisonment.

Terms of Occupation

The speed and strength of the German assault on France caught the French off guard and armed resistance soon collapsed. In their hour of need, they turned to General Pétain, saviour of France during World War I. He quickly signed a peace agreement with Germany that divided the country into two. German troops occupied the north and west, including Paris, while the rest of the country, now governed from Vichy, remained unoccupied.

Occupied France

Within days of the occupation, life returned to normal in most places. In Paris, shops, cafés and restaurants reopened and horse racing resumed. In nightclubs, many bands played to packed audiences of German soldiers and their French girlfriends. Across occupied France, people co-operated – although often reluctantly – with the Germans, although some joined the Resistance (see pages 12–13).

However, the French soon suffered real hardship as German soldiers stripped the markets and shops of food and luxuries such as stockings and perfume. Petrol became almost unobtainable, while a shortage of leather meant many people wore wooden clogs instead of shoes. Food and clothing were rationed, coal and firewood were almost impossible to obtain, and soap became a luxury item.

The Germans enforced a nightly curfew, restricted travel, and imposed censorship. Strikes and demonstrations were forbidden, and enemies were rounded up. Jews suffered particular hardship: in July 1942, French police rounded up 13,000 Jews and deported them to Auschwitz death camp.

Vichy France

General Pétain established a government at Vichy based on order and authority. In theory, this government ran the whole of France and its empire, although in practice, its power was limited to the unoccupied zone. At first, life in this zone continued as before but in November 1942, German troops occupied Vichy France, ending its independence. General Pétain now became the Germans' puppet with no real power.

Nazi officers – some with French girlfriends – enjoy a show in a Paris café in 1940.

Occupied France

May 1940 German armies invade France; Pétain joins the government.

14 June German armies enter Paris.

16 June Pétain becomes prime minister and opens peace talks with Germany.

22 June France agrees armistice with Germany; Germans occupy north and west, Pétain governs rest of France from Vichy.

28 June In London, de Gaulle recognised as leader of Free French by Britain.

Aug 1941 Attacks begin against Jewish properties in Paris.

Mar 1942 First deportation of Jews from occupied France to Auschwitz.

Nov After Allied landings in Vichy-held French North Africa, Germans occupy Vichy France; Pétain continues as German puppet ruler.

6 June 1944 Allied troops land in Normandy to begin liberation of France.

25 August French troops liberate Paris.

September de Gaulle forms new government.

Resistance

As the German armies occupied a country, most people despaired at their nation's defeat and accepted that they were now under foreign rule. Some, however, joined resistance groups to fight for their freedom.

Violette Szabo

Violette Szabo (1921–45), a Londoner, was recruited into the SOE in 1942. Twice she parachuted into France to help set up resistance groups. On her second mission in 1944 she helped the local leader organise sabotage missions but was captured and interrogated by the Germans. Szabo was then sent to the Ravensbruck concentration camp, where she was killed in January 1945.

National Resistance

Resistance groups sprung up across the whole of occupied Europe. They varied considerably from country to country. Some, such as the Milorg in Norway, and the Polish Home Army, were nationalist groups based around their governments in exile in London, while others were based on the pre-war communist parties, which already had extensive underground networks. Resistance groups in western Europe gained help and support from the British Special Operations Executive (SOE), set up to train resistance fighters, organise acts of sabotage and gain intelligence about German troop movements.

The most effective resistance groups were those in countries where the landscape was wild enough to hide in, and where German troops could not operate in large numbers: the mountains of Norway, the forested hills of Czechoslovakia, the mountainous mainland and islands of Greece and Yugoslavia and the more remote parts of France.

Notable Successes

The resistance fighters' successes were considerable: Norwegian fighters flown in from Scotland destroyed the Vermork heavy-water plant, crippling the German atomic weapons programme, while French groups paralysed German communications before the D-Day landings. Armed groups in Yugoslavia and behind German lines in the USSR tied down large numbers of Nazi troops in the latter stages of the war.

An Allied aircraft drops canisters of supplies by parachute to French resistance fighters to keep them equipped in their fight against the Nazis.

❝Set Europe ablaze.❞

British Prime Minister Winston Churchill's instruction to the Special Operations Executive, 16 July 1940

Resistance

June 1940 French resistance groups set up to help Allied airmen escape back to Britain, and Jews to flee to safety in Switzerland or Spain.

July Winston Churchill sets up SOE in London to support European resistance movements.

June 1941 Germany invades USSR: Soviet support now given to communist resistance groups in eastern Europe.

May 1942 Czech resistance fighters assassinate Nazi leader Reinhard Heydrich; Germans kill 5,000 Czechs in revenge.

Feb 1943 Norwegian resistance fighters destroy Vermork heavy-water plant.

June 1944 French resistance groups sabotage German communication systems prior to and after D-Day landings in Normandy; 960 successful attacks carried out.

July French Maquis resistance fighters near Grenoble launch numerous attacks on German troops in the Rhone valley from the Vercors plateau; in response, German troops seal the plateau and kill 850 people.

Aug Polish Home Army leads Warsaw Uprising.

Aug Slovak National Uprising led by SOE-supported resistance fighters put down by German troops with huge loss of life.

Reprisals

The resistance fighters were incredibly brave, sending intelligence back to London and carrying out acts of sabotage and murder at great risk to their own lives. If the Germans caught the fighters, they and their countrymen were often killed in revenge.

In May 1942, two Czech resistance fighters, supported by the SOE, assassinated Reinhard Heydrich, the Nazi ruler of Bohemia and Moravia. In revenge, the Germans shot the two assassins and 100 other resistance fighters; they then murdered the entire population of two nearby villages, Lidice and Lezaky – altogether a total of more than 5,000 people. Other, similar acts of revenge were taken against the French *Maquis* in southern France and the Polish Home Army in Warsaw (see pages 14–15).

Partisans

Across most of Europe, resistance consisted of intelligence gathering, sabotage and other small scale acts of violence. In some places, however, large-scale guerrilla armies, known as partisans, fought the German occupiers.

Many partisan groups, such as these in Yugoslavia, were well organised and equipped and included women fighters.

The Warsaw Uprising

In August 1944, the Polish Home Army – a partisan group supported by the Polish government in exile in London – launched an uprising against the German occupation of Warsaw.

The partisans captured most of the city but were met with savage German reprisals: 10,000 fighters and perhaps 200,000 civilians were killed before the Germans crushed the uprising and razed most of the city to the ground. Controversially, Soviet troops outside the city did not help the partisans, as the USSR supported the rival communist Polish People's Army.

The Partisans

The main areas of partisan activity against German occupation were in Yugoslavia, Albania, behind the German lines in the USSR, and, after 1943, in Italy. All partisan groups were politically motivated and were either communists, or extreme nationalists fighting to restore the pre-war government of their country. The partisans organised themselves into small, highly mobile units and operated in difficult terrain, hiding in remote areas and then attacking German troops, before melting into the background once again to plan their next operation.

Great Success

Partisan warfare was often very successful. The groups operating behind German lines in the USSR had about 250,000 members and reckoned to have wrecked 18,000 trains and killed, wounded, or taken prisoner hundreds of thousands of German soldiers, making life extremely difficult for the Germany army as it struggled to subdue the USSR after its invasion in 1941.

In northern Italy, 200,000 partisans held down thousands of German troops, eventually capturing and killing the former Italian leader Mussolini. In Albania, the communist-led partisans of Enver Hoxha liberated the entire country before the end of the war.

Yugoslavia

The most successful partisan armies operated in Yugoslavia. After the German invasion of the country in April 1941, two main groups led the resistance – the pro-royal, anti-communist Serb Chetniks of Colonel Mihailovic, supported by the British, and the communist-led Yugoslav Partisans of Josip Broz Tito. The two groups fell out with each other for political reasons. When the Chetniks turned to their supposed enemies, Germany and Italy, for support, the British turned to support Tito, supplying him with arms and agents.

By early 1944, Tito had 300,000 partisans and controlled much of the country. As German troops withdrew in the face of the Soviet advance across eastern Europe, the partisans advanced, capturing the capital, Belgrade and eventually forcing the Germans out of the country by the end of the war.

Partisan Warfare

April 1941 Germany invades Yugoslavia, dividing the country with Italy.

Oct 1941 Fighting breaks out between Chetniks and Partisans in Yugoslavia.

May 1942 USSR sets up Central Staff of the Partisan Movement to co-ordinate guerrilla activities behind German lines.

Sept Albanian communists set up National Liberation Movement of partisans to evict Italians.

Sept 1943 Italy signs armistice with the Allies and changes sides in the war; Germany occupies most of country.

Nov Italian anti-fascist partisan groups form Committee of National Liberation to fight German occupation of northern Italy.

Dec British switch support from Chetniks to Partisans in Yugoslavia.

March 1944 Italian partisans call a one-day general strike against German occupation.

Aug 1944 Polish Home Army leads Warsaw Uprising against German occupation.

Oct Albanian partisans liberate their country.

Oct Tito's partisans liberate Yugoslav capital of Belgrade.

April 1945 Italian partisans capture and kill former fascist leader Mussolini.

❝For the towns and villages burnt down, for the death of our women and children, for the torture, violence and humiliation wreaked on my people, I swear to take revenge...❞

Soviet partisan army oath

Undercover

All the nations involved in the war, as well as the many resistance and partisan movements, needed intelligence and information about what the enemy was up to. This intelligence was provided by spies, often working at great risk to their own lives.

This photo shows a German "Enigma" encoding machine in use (at the bottom of the picture). Cracking the Enigma code was the focus of much secret Allied activity in the first half of the war.

Intelligence Gathering

1933 Soviets send Richard Sorge to Tokyo to provide information on Japanese military plans.

1938 Leonard Trepper sets up Red Orchestra in Brussels, later Paris, to spy on western Europe.

July 1940 British set up Special Operations Executive (SOE).

March 1941 Japanese plant Takeo Yoshikawa in Hawaii to provide information about the US naval base at Pearl Harbor.

June Trepper, Sorge and others warn Stalin of German invasion of USSR.

July Sorge sends back information to Moscow about Japanese plans in Asia.

Dec Japanese achieve total surprise when they attack Pearl Harbor, thanks to information supplied by their spy.

May 1942 Czech resistance fighters helped by the SOE, assassinate Reinhard Heydrich, head of the German SD intelligence service.

June Americans set up Office of Strategic Services (OSS).

1943–44 Eleysa Bazna – "Cicero" – Albanian valet to the British ambassador to Turkey, photographs top-secret documents for the SD.

Difficult Conditions

At the start of the war in 1939, Britain, Germany, the USSR and Japan had extensive networks of spies working abroad, although the USA did not. All, however, had to adapt quickly to wartime conditions, especially after Germany and Japan overran so much territory, making it difficult for British and American agents to operate safely on the ground.

In 1940, the British set up a new secret service, the Special Operations Executive (SOE) to combine intelligence gathering with secret operations abroad. The Americans set up the similar Office of Strategic Services (OSS) in 1942. Together these two organisations, working with local resistance and partisan groups, caused chaos behind enemy lines in both Europe and Asia.

Soviet Mistrust

Although the USSR ran the largest network of spies, its leader, Josef Stalin, did not always trust the information he received. Leopold Trepper – the leader of the "Red Orchestra" European spy network in Paris – and Richard Sorge, a half-German Russian spy who worked in Japan, both sent back information that Germany was about to invade the USSR in 1941. Stalin did not believe them and refused to act until it was too late.

Stalin also refused to believe information from Sorge in July 1941 that the Japanese were planning a military campaign in southeast Asia rather than against the USSR. This information should have allowed Stalin to move thousands of troops away from defensive duties in the eastern USSR to fight the Germans in the west. In this case, however, Stalin later changed his mind when decoded messages confirmed Sorge's information, and he shifted troops west in time to defend Moscow.

German Successes

The Germans ran two intelligence services, the *Abwehr*, attached to the armed services, and the *Sicherheitsdienst* (SD), attached to the SS (see glossary). The SD used Jewish workers in concentration camps to forge large numbers of British banknotes in an effort to break the British economy, and ran an agent – "Cicero" – in the British embassy in neutral Turkey. Cicero gained information about meetings between the Allied leaders in Moscow, Cairo and Teheran and details of the forthcoming D-Day allied invasion of Europe in June 1944, although the SD mishandled the information and little benefit was gained.

Enigma

One of the greatest successes of the war was the British breaking of German secret codes. The Germans used a machine known as Enigma to code and send all their top-secret messages.

To break the codes, the British got together a group of experts – including Alan Turing, the "father" of modern computers – at Bletchley Park outside London. Here they developed machines called bombes that helped them understand how Enigma worked and thus decipher its messages.

This information saved thousands of lives and possibly shortened the war by months. Extraordinarily, the Germans never realised that their secret codes had been broken and that the British were reading all their military messages.

The Enigma machine. Messages typed into it by the operator were automatically encoded; the code was extremely difficult to break without another machine.

Eastern Europe

When they occupied western Europe, the Germans had some respect for the peoples who lived there and on the whole treated them reasonably well. In eastern Europe, however, the Germans viewed the people there as sub-humans, and inflicted terrible suffering on them.

The Holocaust

The Nazi Party was deeply anti-Semitic. Once in power in Germany in 1933, it began to discriminate against Jews, removing their civil rights, destroying their synagogues and businesses, and attacking them in the streets.

After the Germans invaded Poland and then the USSR, millions more Jews came under German rule. The Nazis then devised the "Final Solution of the Jewish question", that is their extermination in death camps such as Auschwitz.

By the time the war ended in 1945, the Nazis had killed six million Jews – more than half the total Jewish population of Europe and one-third of all Jews in the world. Today we call this genocide against Jewish people the Holocaust.

Racial Supremacy

Adolf Hitler and his Nazi Party believed the Germans were an "Aryan" (fair-haired, fair-skinned) master race, who should rule the world. Danes, Norwegians and Dutch – all similar-looking to the Germans – and other western Europeans were therefore treated with some respect, providing they did not rebel. However, the Nazis considered the peoples of eastern Europe – the Slavs of Poland and Russia, and above all the Jews – as sub-humans who could be cleared away to make *Lebensraum* (living room) for the German master race. The Nazi occupation of this region was therefore marked with appalling brutality and terror, with millions loosing their lives.

Death and Destruction

As the German armies swept into Poland and then later the USSR, the *Einsatzgruppen* (special units of the SS) followed the troops. They shot all communists, many Jews and other "enemies" on the spot. The scale of this killing was immense – 40,000 German soldiers, supported by German policemen and local Nazi sympathisers, killed nearly 500,000 Jews in the three Baltic states and in Belarus and Ukraine in 1941 alone. Thousands of Polish and Russian civilians were also shot and many more evicted from their homes to make room for German settlers. Those Jews who were not shot were herded into ghettos.

Death Camps

The violence directed at the Poles, Russians and other people was widespread but disorganised. Nazi policy towards the Jews, however, was deliberate – all Jews were eventually to be killed, an act of genocide we call the Holocaust (see box). At first, eastern European Jews were shot, or killed in mobile gas vans, but both these methods were too slow to cope with the millions of Jews living in the area, as well as those Jews living in German-occupied western and southern Europe. As a result, the Nazis built five death camps – the most notorious of which was Auschwitz – which together killed 2.6 million Jews and perhaps another 500,000 Russians, Poles, gypsies and prisoners of war, on an industrial scale.

Nazi tanks and troops attack a Jewish ghetto in Poland, 1943.

Eastern Europe

Sept 1939 Germany invades Poland.

Oct First Jewish ghetto set up in Piotrkow, Poland.

Nov Warsaw ghetto established.

June 1941 Germany invades USSR.

Oct 22,000 Jews taken from Germany to Polish ghettos, the first of many such transports.

Dec First death camp opened at Chelmno, Poland.

Jan 1942 Nazis hold Wannsee Conference to plan the "Final Solution of the Jewish question".

Mar Germans begin to clear Jews out of the ghettos and move them east for "resettlement", that is murder or work in the labour camps.

Mar First Jews taken by train to their deaths in Auschwitz.

May First gassings occur at Auschwitz.

Jan 1943 German army surrenders at Stalingrad, the furthest extent of German occupation of USSR.

July 1944 Soviet Red Army begins liberation of Poland.

Jan 1945 Red Army liberates Auschwitz.

Forced Labour

Throughout the war, Germany forced large numbers of people to work producing materials for the war effort. Most of these labourers were treated like slaves, and many died of overwork, maltreatment or hunger.

Thailand–Burma Railway

The Japanese used forced labour to build a 415-km (258-mile) railway between Thailand and Burma, much of it running alongside the Kwai Nok river. More than 61,000 British, Dutch, American and Australian prisoners of war, alongside thousands of Chinese, Malay and Burmese workers, were forced to build the railway through thick jungle and along treacherous mountain ridges.

The Japanese treated the workers brutally, making them work from dawn to dusk in extreme heat or monsoon rains. By the time the railway was completed in October 1943, 12,000 prisoners of war and 90,000 Asian workers were dead, one for each 4 m (13 ft) of track.

Feeding the War

Throughout the war, German industry required vast numbers of workers to produce arms, ammunition, tanks, jeeps, airplanes, chemicals, steel, cement and other items for the war effort. Labourers were also needed to work in quarries and mines to produce the raw materials industry demanded and to work on the land to grow food. All fit and available German men, however, were fighting in the armed services, so vast numbers of foreign and other labourers were forced to do the work instead.

Slave Labourers

These forced or slave labourers were drawn from four groups: prisoners of war; concentration camp inmates, including criminals, gypsies and enemies

Half-starved Allied prisoners of the Japanese work on the Thailand-Burma railway.

of the state; Jews, Poles, Russians and others from the eastern territories; and large numbers of civilians from occupied western Europe. In total, by 1944 more than 5.3 million civilians and 1.8 million prisoners of war were working against their will for the Germans.

The German firms that used forced or slave labour included such well-known names as the Krupp arms manufacturers, the Heinkel, Junkers and Messerschmitt aircraft builders, the Siemens and Telefunken electrical businesses, and the BMW and Daimler-Benz motor manufacturers, who produced armoured cars and aircraft engines.

New arrivals on the railway platform at Auschwitz queue up for "selection". A bleak fate awaited them: death in the gas chambers or, for the fit, forced labour.

Working to Death

Most slave labourers lived in labour or prisoner of war camps and were marched under guard to and from work each day. New factories – such as the I.G. Farben petrochemical works outside the Auschwitz III labour camp – were built next to the camps to make use of their available labour.

The treatment slave labourers received varied according to their skills and racial background. Skilled workers always received better treatment than unskilled labourers, while French or Dutch workers, for example, were treated better than Russians, Poles or, worst of all, Jews. How many labourers lost their lives for Germany is not known, but more than three million Russian workers died, as did 30,000 others who worked for I.G. Farben.

❝ *Every month one-fifth died or were, because of inability to work, sent back … to the camps … to be exterminated.* ❞

Rudolf Höss, commandant of Auschwitz III labour camp

Life in Hitler's Reich

Opposition

Most Germans were not Nazis but supported Hitler because they were German patriots. Others opposed the war: 4,000 students in Munich rioted when the district governor accused them of failing to fight for their country, while a few Christian churchmen, notably Pastor Dietrich Bonhöffer, were brave enough to preach against Nazi persecution of the Jews and other peoples, or even organise against them. Two assassination attempts were made against Hitler before a group of high-ranking army officers came close to killing him in 1944. Nazi intelligence, however, crushed most resistance before it could have any effect.

The war affected not just occupied Europe but Germany, too. Most Germans supported the war, although they were fearful about its outcome, but some opposed the Nazis and felt that they, too, were under occupation by a foreign power.

Life as Normal

Most people in Germany – except those fighting abroad in the armed services – were unaffected by the outbreak of war. Life carried on as usual, despite the introduction of food and petrol rationing and a night-time blackout on all lights. Poor people were given special food allowances at lower prices, and probably enjoyed a better diet that they had in peacetime. Everyone in Germany benefited from the occupation of western Europe in 1940: supplies

Hitler surveys the damage to his headquarters from the bomb that nearly killed him in July 1944.

of Dutch dairy produce, French stockings and perfume, and Norwegian furs flooded into the country. People continued to take holidays by the sea or in the mountains, cinemas and theatres remained open, and almost all women continued to stay at home and not go out to work.

Life Gets Worse

This situation changed for the worse in the winter of 1941–42. Germany began to run out of food because so many farm workers were now fighting in the USSR. Bread and meat rations were cut and the daily diet became poorer. The Allied bombing of German cities killed thousands and made many more homeless. In Berlin, every third house was completely destroyed or uninhabitable, while 800,000 people – two-thirds of the total German population – had to be evacuated from Hamburg after the Allies flattened the city in 1943.

Total War

After the massive German defeat at Stalingrad in February 1943, Josef Goebbels, the German propaganda minister, announced "total war" measures in order to win the war. All men aged between 16 and 65 were registered for compulsory labour, youths aged 10 to 15 were sent to help out on the farms, and millions of women were conscripted to work in industry and civil defence. By the end of the war, rations had been cut again and again, food was scarce, and the looting of food stores and freight trains became common.

Wartime Germany

Sept 1939 Food and petrol rationing introduced at outbreak of war; compulsory one-year service, mostly in agriculture, for unmarried women under 25.

Nov Clothes rationing introduced.

April–June 1940 Occupation of western Europe brings in new foodstuffs and luxury items.

June 1941 Bread and meat rations cut.

Winter 1941–42 Food shortages occur as farmworkers fight on the eastern front and railway wagons now used to transport military supplies, not food.

May 1942 First Allied 1,000 bomber raid on Cologne.

Feb 1943 German army suffers massive defeat at Stalingrad in Russia; Goebbels announces "total war" measures.

Feb Munich students shout down the district governor, leading to anti-Nazi demonstrations and riots.

July Hamburg flattened by Allied bombs.

July 1944 "July Bomb plot" fails to assassinate Hitler with a bomb in his headquarters.

Sept Women conscripted into industry.

❝ *Do you know that in future teeth are going to be pulled through the nose?"*
"Why?"
"Because nobody dares open his mouth! **❞**

One of the many anti-Nazi Flusterwitze (whispered jokes) circulating in Germany during the war

Under the Rising Sun

A platoon of Japanese soldiers in an invasion craft, with their distinctive "rising sun" flag.

Resistance Movements

After the initial welcome given to the invaders, resistance groups formed to fight the Japanese.

Filipino troops that refused to surrender to the Japanese in 1942 retreated into the jungles and more remote islands, from where they attacked Japanese troops. In Vietnam, the Viet Minh movement raided Japanese forces and sent intelligence to the Americans, while the Burmese National Army – which had previously supported the Japanese against their British colonial rulers – changed sides and declared war against Japan.

Japan's control of its southeast-Asian empire remained firm, however, until Japan itself was forced to surrender in 1945.

The Japanese conquest of southeast Asia brought 150 million people under Japanese rule. Unlike in Europe, however, most of these peoples welcomed their invaders as liberators.

Co-operation

In Europe, Germany and Italy invaded and occupied independent nations. However, this was not true of Japan in Asia, for with the exception of China, Japan occupied European or American colonies, such as British Malaya, the Dutch East Indies, and the American Philippines. As a result, many Asian peoples saw Japan as an Asian liberator from colonial rule, and they welcomed its invading armies with open arms.

Japan had already planned how to run its new empire, setting up a Greater East Asia Co-Prosperity Sphere to promote economic co-operation in the region and end its dependence on Europe and America. Where possible, local leaders ran the former colonies, two of which were even granted independence by the Japanese.

Control

The reality, however, was that Japan remained in full control. The entire Japanese Empire kept to local Tokyo time, flew the Japanese rising sun flag and used Japanese money. Children learned Japanese, the use of western languages was prohibited – although English continued to be used as the common language in most places – and American music and films were banned. All public meetings began with a bow to the Japanese emperor, non-approved political parties were outlawed and newspapers censored. Everyone carried an identity card and needed a special pass to travel anywhere.

Brutality

Japanese rule was often very brutal. Japanese troops massacred more than 250,000 civilians when they captured the Chinese capital, Nanking, in 1937, and killed many thousands more across southeast Asia. All prisoners of war were treated with great cruelty (see pages 26–27). Everywhere the *Kempeitai* (military police) kept order with beatings and torture: victims were hung by their wrists and tortured with electricity and chemicals.

The Japanese also stripped their empire of food, war materials and labour. All men aged 16 to 40 and single women aged 16 to 25 were rounded up in the Dutch East Indies, Malaya and Burma and put to work in factories or farms or made to build railways and roads (see page 20). Those left in the villages faced great hardship, as most able-bodied people were no longer there to work on the land. As a result, food became scarce, and famine broke out: at least 400,000 Vietnamese lost their lives in 1944–45, as did many more in the Philippines and Malaya.

Japanese Occupation

Sept 1931 Japanese seize Chinese province of Manchuria.

July 1937 Japanese invade rest of China.

Dec 250,000 Chinese massacred by Japanese after capture of Nanking.

Nov 1938 Japanese establish Greater East Asia Co-Prosperity Sphere.

July 1941 Japanese occupy bases in French Indo-China (Vietnam) and dominate the country; Viet Minh resistance movement formed.

Dec Japanese attack Pearl Harbor, Malaya, Philippines and Hong Kong; Thailand co-operates with the Japanese government.

Jan 1942 Japanese invade Dutch East Indies and Burma.

Feb Japanese set up Greater Asia Council with representatives from its conquered empire.

Aug Japanese declare Burma independent, followed by Philippines in October.

Nov 1943 Greater East Asia Conference of local rulers meets in Tokyo.

March 1945 Burmese National Army declares war on Japan.

Aug Americans drop atomic bombs on Japanese cities of Hiroshima and Nagasaki.

Sept Japanese surrender to American forces, ending the war in Asia.

66 *Asia for the Asians.* 99

Japanese slogan

Prisoners of War

As the tides of war washed across Europe and Asia, both sides took vast numbers of prisoners. The conditions under which these prisoners lived were often appalling.

Changi

One of the most brutal prison camps was at Changi on Singapore Island. Here the Japanese kept 50,000 British and Commonwealth PoWs captured after the fall of Singapore in February 1942.

At first the prisoners looked after themselves, as they had no place to escape to and were thus no danger, but gradually conditions deteriorated. Food became scarce and by the end of the war, the inmates were eating seaweed and whatever food they could scavenge. Many of the men were sent to work, and die, building roads and other projects.

In total, 8,000 of the 22,000 Australian prisoners and 12,500 of the 50,000 British prisoners captured by the Japanese during the war died at their hands.

Interned

At the outbreak of war, large numbers of people living abroad immediately became enemy aliens and were interned in camps or deported to other countries. In Britain 74,000 Germans and Austrians were detained – even though many were Jewish refugees fleeing Nazi persecution – and sent to camps on the Isle of Man in Britain or deported to Canada or Australia. In December 1941, 124,000 Germans and 50,000 Italians living in the USA were similarly detained in camps when the USA entered the war. In both Britain and the USA the detainees were treated well, and many were quickly released when their loyalty to their new country was confirmed.

The Geneva Convention

Prisoners captured on the battlefield were treated far less well. All prisoners of war (PoWs) were protected under the Geneva Convention of 1929, which guaranteed that the prisoners received food, clothing, medical treatment, regular exercise and the right to receive letters and parcels. The convention also set out the maximum penalty of 30 days' solitary confinement if they tried to escape. However, neither the USSR nor Japan had signed the convention, which meant any PoWs they kept, and their nationals kept by other nations, were treated far worse.

Colditz

One of the most famous prison camps in Germany was Oflag IV C in Saxony, better known as Colditz Castle. Colditz stood on a cliff high above a river and its guards outnumbered the prisoners.

Allied officer PoWs were sent here after attempting to escape from other German prison camps, for the castle was meant to be escape-proof. That did not stop the prisoners: "Every officer in this castle had but a single thought – to escape," wrote one inmate, Lt Airey Neave, later a British MP. Six Dutch officers got out through a manhole cover in the yard, while a Scot was smuggled out in a straw prison mattress. One group of inmates even built a 10-metre (33-foot) wide glider in the attic, although it never flew as the war was ending by the time it was ready. In all, more than 60 prisoners escaped, the highest record of successful escapes anywhere in Nazi Germany.

A Personal Story

John Hipkin was 14 years old when his ship, the SS *Lustrous*, was sunk off Canada and he was taken prisoner – the youngest British PoW of World War II. He spent four years in a German camp. "It was a dumping ground for … all the defeated countries of Europe. What you have to remember is that they had German prisoners in Britain, so we were treated well because otherwise their troops would suffer. But for the Russians, there was no quarter given. They were literally allowed to starve to death."

Colditz Castle prison was meant to be escape-proof.

Liberation

Starting with the Allied invasion of Italy in July 1943, the Allies slowly began to liberate Europe and Asia from German, Italian and Japanese rule. The cost in human lives was high, while the price of peace was often far higher.

War Crimes Trials

After the war, leading Nazis charged with war crimes were put on trial at Nuremberg. An International Military Tribunal tried 21 Nazis, 11 of whom were sentenced to death. Trials of lesser Nazis have continued to this day. In Japan, seven wartime leaders, including Prime Minister Tojo, were hanged while 16 others were sentenced to life imprisonment.

The main culprits escaped justice: Hitler commited suicide, Mussolini was killed by partisans, and Emperor Hirohito of Japan renounced his divine status and became a constitutional monarch until his death in 1989.

Western Europe

The invasion of Italy in July 1943 led to the overthrow of Mussolini's government and the reintroduction of democratic rule in Italy. However, the Germans quickly occupied the centre and north of Italy, enslaving Italians in their own country. Partisan groups then fought the Germans, a conflict that went on until the end of the war.

In France, the Allied invasion led to the ending of Vichy rule and the reintroduction of democratic government led by General de Gaulle. About 10,500 people were executed for collaboration – either by the courts or by the Resistance – and another 40,000 sent to prison.

Free French leader General Charles de Gaulle enters Paris on 25 August 1944.

In Belgium, the government returned from exile in London to take control, while King Leopold III, taken prisoner by the Germans in 1944, was forbidden to return until 1950, as many Belgians accused him of collaboration.

Eastern Europe

The situation in eastern Europe was far more complex as the Soviets wanted to replace the previous governments with communist regimes. Although the Czech government returned from exile in London, and the kings of Romania and Bulgaria remained in place, pro-Soviet communist republics were established through the region by 1948. In Yugoslavia, Tito and his partisans took power but soon broke with the USSR to pursue a more independent line. In Greece, civil war broke out between royalist and communist partisans that ended in a royalist victory in 1949.

Asia

The USA decided that it would take too long to push the Japanese out of their conquests in southeast Asia. Instead it decided to attack Japan itself, dropping two atomic bombs in an effort to bomb Japan out of the war. As a result, Japanese troops remained throughout southeast Asia with the exception of the Philippines and western Burma until after the Japanese surrender in September 1945. Although the Europeans and Americans returned to rule their colonies, independence was granted first to Burma and then to Indonesia and the rest of the region.

Liberation

July 1943 Liberation of Italy begins.

Sept Italy signs armistice with Allies and changes sides in war.

June 1944 D-Day: Allies land in Normandy to begin liberation of France.

July Soviet Red Army clears German army out of USSR.

Aug Red Army liberates Romania and then Bulgaria.

Sept Allies liberate Belgium and Luxembourg.

Oct British liberate Greece, Tito's Partisans liberate most of Yugoslavia, USA begins invasion of the Philippines.

Feb 1945 Red Army liberates Poland and enters Germany.

Mar Allies cross Rhine to begin liberation of Germany and Netherlands; US captures Japanese island of Iwo Jima.

April Red Army liberates Hungary and much of Czechoslovakia.

April Death of Hitler on 30 April brings German surrender on 7 May and the end of war in Europe.

June USA captures Japanese island of Okinawa.

Aug Atomic bombs dropped on Japanese cities of Hiroshima and Nagasaki.

Sept Japan surrenders, bringing war in Asia to an end.

Liberation was marked with rejoicing, as here in Paris. But the war produced millions of homeless refugees, bombed-out cities and shattered economies.

Glossary

Ally A country linked with another by treaty, friendship or common military purpose.

Allies, the USA, USSR, Britain, France and their allies in the war against Germany, Italy and Japan.

Anti-Semitism Prejudice against Jewish people.

Armistice An agreement between opposing sides to cease fire while a peace agreement is agreed.

Civilian A person whose main occupation is civil or non-military.

Code A system for hiding a message by replacing whole words or phrases with one or more letters, numbers or symbols.

Collaborator Someone who works with the enemy.

Communism The belief in a society that exists without different social classes and in which everyone is equal and all property is owned by the people.

Death camp Also called an extermination camp, where Jews and others were systematically killed, usually by poison gas.

Democracy Government by the people or their elected representatives, often forming opposing political parties.

Dictatorship Government by a leader who takes complete control of a country and often rules by force.

Einsatzgruppen "Action groups": special squads of SS officers ordered to kill enemies of the state, notably Jews and communists in occupied Poland and Russia.

Empire A group of different nations and peoples, ruled by one nation and its emperor or leader.

Fascism Extreme political movement based on nationalism and authority, often military, which aims to unite a country's people into a disciplined force under an all-powerful leader; Mussolini's Fascist Party ruled Italy from 1922–43.

Genocide The deliberate destruction of a racial, religious, political or ethnic group.

Ghetto Poor part of a town or city where Jews were forced to live, often walled off from the rest of the town.

Guerrilla Member of an unofficial, usually politically motivated, armed force.

Hitler, Adolf (1889–1945) Leader of the German Nazi Party 1921–45, and ruler of Germany 1933–45.

Holocaust The deliberate attempt by Nazis to kill all Jews in Europe.

Labour camp A camp using slave labour, mostly Jews and prisoners of war, to produce materials for the German war effort.

Nationalist A person who is passionately loyal and devoted to his or her own country.

Nazi Party The extreme fascist party of Adolf Hitler that ruled Germany from 1933–45.

Neutral A nation that refuses to take sides in a war and does not fight.

Partisan A member of an armed resistance group fighting inside a country against an invading or occupying army.

Red Army Army of the USSR.

Reich The German word for "empire"; Hitler's Germany was often called the Third Reich, as it followed two previous German empires.

Republic A country governed by an elected head of state called a president.

SS, the *Schutzstaffel* or "protection squads", originally set up to protect senior members of the Nazi Party but later developed into the organisation responsible for the *Einsatzgruppen* and the death camps.

Treaty A formal agreement between two or more countries.

USSR Union of the Soviet Socialist Republics, or the Soviet Union, which existed from 1922–91; commonly known as Russia.

WEBSITES

www.spartacus.schoolnet.co.uk/2WW.htm Comprehensive site covering every aspect of World War II, including entries on the Special Operations Executive, the French and other resistance movements and their key members, spies and spying, and codes and ciphers.

www.bbc.co.uk/history/war/wwtwo/index.shtml Official BBC site on the war, with numerous photographs, maps, and spoken word extracts, including entries on the SOE and partisans.

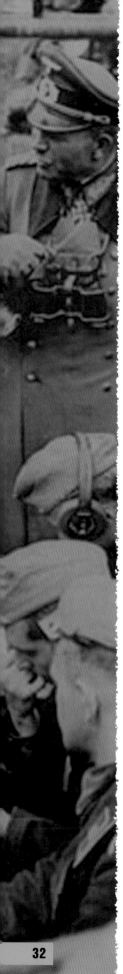

Index